Sacred Solos
Level Two

Supplement to All Piano and Keyboard Methods
Compiled, Arranged, and Edited by Wesley Schaum

Foreword

This series of sacred solos includes favorite hymns, gospel songs, spirituals and sacred music from the classical repertoire. The selections have been made to appeal to students of all ages and also with regard to popularity in many different churches. Some of the hymn tunes may be known with different titles and lyrics.

Duet accompaniments offer many possibilities for recitals and Sunday school participation. The duets help provide valuable rhythmic training and ensemble experience. Duets are recommended for use at home as well as at the lesson. The person playing the accompaniment is free to add pedal according to his/her own taste.

Contents

PLAYBACK+
Speed • Pitch • Balance • Loop

To access audio, visit:
www.halleonard.com/mylibrary

4037-5583-9642-8620

ISBN 978-1-4950-8216-0

Schaum

EXCLUSIVELY DISTRIBUTED BY

HAL•LEONARD®

Visit Hal Leonard Online at
www.halleonard.com

Contact Us:
Hal Leonard
7777 West Bluemound Road
Milwaukee, WI 53213
Email: info@halleonard.com

In Europe contact:
Hal Leonard Europe Limited
Distribution Centre, Newmarket Road
Bury St Edmunds, Suffolk, IP33 3YB
Email: info@halleonardeurope.com

In Australia contact:
Hal Leonard Australia Pty. Ltd.
4 Lentara Court
Cheltenham, Victoria, 3192 Australia
Email: info@halleonard.com.au

Duet Accompaniment

Notes with *stems up* are to be played with the *right* hand. Notes with *stems down* are to be played with the *left* hand.

Jesus Shall Reign

Isaac Watts

John Hatton

Duet Accompaniment

Dynamic markings in the duet accompaniments are the same as in the solo part, so they can be used as reference points during rehearsal. However, the duet part should ***always be played softer*** so that the melody may be heard clearly.

Kum Ba Yah

African-American Spiritual

Duet Accompaniment

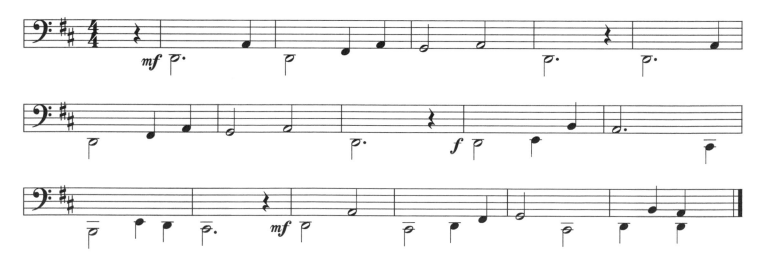

All Glory, Laud and Honor

Theodulph of Orleans   **Melchoir Teschner**

Maestoso

How Great Thou Art

Swedish Folk Song
Arr. by John W. Schaum

Andantino

Al - might - y God, In Thy dear pres - ence kneel - ing,

I come to Thee. My heart is filled with love.

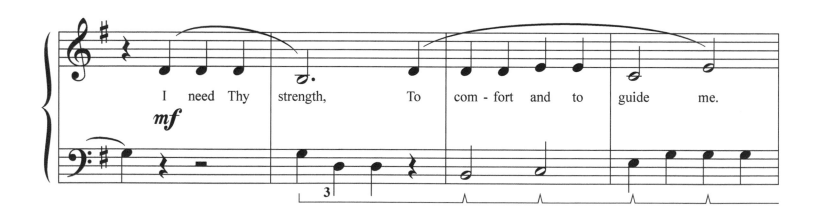

I need Thy strength, To com - fort and to guide me.

I trust in Thee, The com - pass of my life.

Just As I Am

Charlotte Elliott

William B. Bradbury

come,   I   come!

mp

Duet Accompaniment

Duet Accompaniment

Hosanna, Loud Hosanna

Jeanette Threlfall

Herzogl Songbook

Crown Him With Many Crowns

Matthew Bridges   George J. Elvey

Allelujah

Mozart, K165

Duet Accompaniment

Swing Low, Sweet Chariot

African-American Spiritual

A Mighty Fortress Is Our God

Martin Luther

Martin Luther

Maestoso

Duet Accompaniment

seek to work us woe. His craft and pow'r are great, And

armed with cru - el hate, On earth is not his e - qual.

He's Got The Whole World In His Hands

African-American Spiritual

in His___ hands, He's got the whole world in His hands.

Duet Accompaniment

Pachelbel's Canon

Johann Pachelbel

Andante espressivo

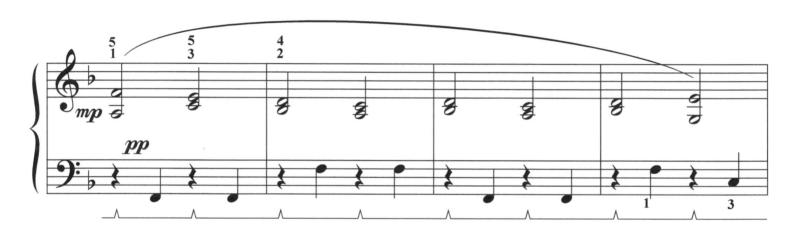

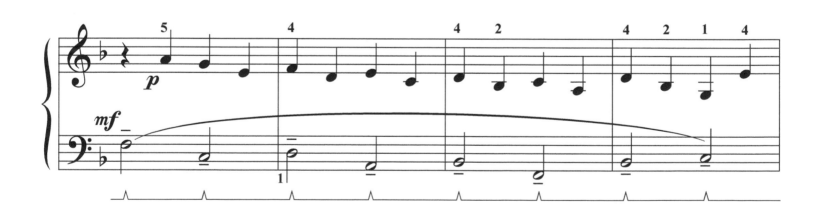

MORE GREAT SCHAUM PUBLICATIONS

FINGERPOWER®

by John W. Schaum
Physical training and discipline
are needed for both athletics and
keyboard playing. Keyboard muscle
conditioning is called technic.
Technic exercises are as important
to the keyboard player as workouts
and calisthenics are to the athlete.
Schaum's *Fingerpower®* books
are dedicated to development
of individual finger strength and
dexterity in both hands.

00645334	Primer Level – Book Only	$6.99
00645016	Primer Level – Book/Audio	$8.99
00645335	Level 1 – Book Only	$6.99
00645019	Level 1 – Book/Audio	$7.99
00645336	Level 2 – Book Only	$6.99
00645022	Level 2 – Book/Audio	$7.99
00645337	Level 3 – Book Only	$6.95
00645025	Level 3 – Book/Audio	$7.99
00645338	Level 4 – Book Only	$6.99
00645028	Level 4 – Book/Audio	$8.99
00645339	Level 5 Book Only	$6.99
00645340	Level 6 Book Only	$6.99

FINGERPOWER® ETUDES

Melodic exercises crafted by master
technic composers. Modified or
transposed etudes provide equal
hand development with a planned
variety of technical styles, key, and
time signatures.

00645392	Primer Level	$6.95
00645393	Level 1	$6.99
00645394	Level 2	$6.99
00645395	Level 3	$6.95
00645396	Level 4	$6.99

FINGERPOWER® FUN

arr. Wesley Schaum
Early Elementary Level
Musical experiences beyond the
traditional *Fingerpower®* books that
include fun to play pieces with finger
exercises and duet accompaniments.
Short technic prepartory drills (finger
workouts) focus on melodic patterns
found in each piece.

00645126	Primer Level	$6.95
00645127	Level 1	$6.95
00645128	Level 2	$6.95
00645129	Level 3	$6.95
00645144	Level 4	$6.95

FINGERPOWER POP

Arranged by James Poteat
10 great pop piano solo
arrangements with fun technical
warm-ups that complement the
Fingerpower series! Can also be used
as motivating supplements to any
method and in any learning situation.

00237508	Primer Level	$9.99
00237510	Level 1	$9.99
00282865	Level 2	$9.99

FINGERPOWER® TRANSPOSER

by Wesley Schaum
Early Elementary Level
This book includes 21 short,
8-measure exercises using 5-finger
patterns. Positions are based on C,F,
and G major and no key signatures
are used. Patterns involve intervals
of 3rds, 4ths, and 5ths up and down
and are transposed from C to F and
F to C, C to G and G to C, G to F and
F to G.

00645150	Primer Level	$6.95
00645151	Level 1	$6.95
00645152	Level 2	$6.95
00645154	Level 3	$6.95
00645156	Level 4	$6.95

JUMBO STAFF MANUSCRIPT BOOK

This pad features 24 pages with 4
staves per page.
00645936 . . . . $4.25

CERTIFICATE OF MUSICAL ACHIEVEMENT

Reward your students for their hard
work with these official 8x10 inch
certificates that you can customize.
12 per package.
00645938 . . . . $6.99

SCHAUM LESSON ASSIGNMENT BOOK

by John Schaum
With space for 32 weeks, this book
will help keep students on the right
track for their practice time.
00645935 . . . . $3.95

HAL•LEONARD®
www.halleonard.com